Spirit of the Vale

Poems from Nature and life In the Vale of Evesham

Bob Woodroofe

Greenwood Press

First published in 2000

This impression 2019

Greenwood Press
38 Birch Avenue
Evesham
Worcs WR11 1YJ

Tel : 01386 446477

http://greenwoodpress.co.uk

ISBN 978-0-9521165-2-3

Introduction

This is the third in the trilogy of poetry collections inspired by nature and life in the Vale of Evesham.

Each collection shows the changes in life both in the Vale and in the writer himself.

Bob Woodroofe 2000

Contents

Rehearsal

Streamside Alder burnt sienna catkinned.
Breast quivers light, piping Spring.

Repeat note, perfect performance, tune replay.
Reeds gleam, fluid tones ring over water gloom.

Flutes, phrases uttered, whistle showers.
Waves recited, flowing together.

Pouring forth soul to sky.
River echoes pure reprise.

Drop from branch. Voice winged away.
Recital over. Silence streams.

Stamping Ground

Just another crop, we grew here,
like the orchard where we scrumped Worcesters.
The strawberry field we raided, the rhubarb patch
where we secretly sucked the sharp pink stems,
and the plums galore, all in season.

We knew every field, hedge, birds nest.
'Three tree corner', the 'pigway' complete with sty,
where the pig munched on sprays of elm.
Willows for bows, elder for arrows,
strings of bird scarers for explosives.

Rolled a dumped tyre down 'Blaney's Lane',
hit a car, hid when the driver chased us.
Dropped stones down the well, long seconds,
one, two, three, four, five, splash.
Pennies on the line for the L.M.S. to squash.

Tried to ride cows, enticed with grass,
climbed on from the gate, quickly thrown.
Sledged into sprout fields, crashed into stems,
slid wildly across flood meadows, dragging feet
to stop before we reached thin ice near the river.

We knew every pond and stream
for frogspawn, loach and minnow.
The river for perch, chub and pike.
Fishing by touch in dead of night.
Writhing eels torched on the bank.

Plop of vole, skitter of water hen,
owls screech across misted fields.
De Montfort's ghosts remain,
haunting 'Dead Man's Ait',
just as ours will, one day.

Sentry

Always a distant view,
tight essed neck,
you hang, hooked to sky.

Gaunt streamside sentinel,
ever vigilant,
ghosts along water's edge.

Languid strokes beat and glide
angular legs unsheathe
dangle on wings that brake air.

You alight, softly, stand in
silent stealth, gold orbed eye
beads water, patient wait.

In a blur the S uncoils,
daggers the air,
splinters mirrored image.

Beak speared, living silver flashes,
juggled, gulped down,
taken in, like you never are.

Alchemy

Air at dew point, water weighted,
pores secrete tears.
Held by a hair's breadth,
clear crystal perfect
reflective spheres
sparkled by a wind's waft,
mirror blue from flower's bed.

Blooms without petals, 8 winged stars,
cluster in tiny galaxies.
Haired velvet of toothed green
pleated with strong veins.
Cloaks that fold through the dark,
cover Transylvanian links,
spread silver from mountain moon.

From philosopher's stone,
prime element of creation,
poured from your leaves.
The summit of perfection,
celestial water, elixir of life,
transmute to perfect metal.
Our Lady's mantle.

V

You hear them first,
the plaintive sound breaks,
echoes off cloud banks,
binding them together.

Search sky for undulating skein
that rises above roll of hill,
crosses the river, passes
over gold waves of wheat.

Spirit lifts like air over wing
as tuned in harmonic flight,
stepped in rhythmic ease
they beat home to roost.

Sun lights passing pinions,
the brown of Canadas,
but one is snow,
miles from home.

Pretence

Delicate paleness forces
through concrete ground.
Fragile shoot of softest cream
blooms at harvest, unadorned,
opens into mauve beauty,
lilac lined flecked with white.

Frenchmen call you “cul tout nu”
but you are too pure for that.
“Naked ladies” is more apt.
Fallow of bare earth between
the glossiness of green skirts
spring breezes lift each year.

Poison lily of damp fields
in season but falsely named,
a flavour of yellow colour,
dye from orange stigmas ground.
Insubstantial as petals
dashed to pieces by the rain.

Summer's End

I've noticed you,
these last few days,
sat on the wire,
telling summer's story
to your children.
Sun soaked days,
soaring high over the earth
on arced wings,
or skimming ground for food
in thunder showers,
exploding crystal rain drops
that ball and roll off oiled plumage.
Gathering strength for the journey,
storing it away to last,
to fuel the flight
that instinct senses.
One last twitter
as if goodbye,
slim body tenses,
you launch yourself,
gleaming blue steel,
circle once and away south,
trailing feather streamers.

Marquis fined £5,000

From night's peace saw sun hover
over steaming water, burn away mist
with golden laser, reeds flick light
into breeze from fan of passing tail.
Bubbles fizz, pop through surface skin

Lily pad tremor circles onto calm
from blunt head of feeding Carp,
Rudd drift, suck flies from film.
Perch dash, fins ablaze,
chase Minnows through shallows.

Swept away in creeping tide,
silent froth of filth, float
belly up, flesh putrid, stinking
pitiful heap, buried out of sight.
Scale scum glistens, all that remains.

Goldfinch

Greet me so bold.
With flash of gold meet me.
Roam from head to head
light winged on the breeze.
Cast ideas like thistledown,
parachuting, seeding air.
Sun rays of hope,
seeking dreams.
Seeking the seed
to split open, prize out
the precious grain
to fuel such a bright
bundle of coloured life.
Discard the empty shell.
Husk on the wind.
Twist and turn,
this way and that,
wafted by the mind's breeze,
buffeted by wind and wing.
Emerge unscathed,
settle and take root,
grow into being,
bloom to maturity.
Turn to solid
from featherlight,
realise the dream.

Keeping Watch

The air hangs still, expectant,
drinks the green.
Feel it push up, hear it grow,
taste the fresh juicy blade.

Primroses glow from dappled bank,
a peacock velvets down the ride,
settles, sucks blackthorn dew.
Hand layered stone sunlights the way.

The old quarry now bathed in green,
drowned in lark's song, betrays the hill's origin.
Quartzed coral and shell weathered
by the elements from honeyed rock.

Sheep snuffle across the ridge,
crop the short turf even closer,
startle with fright at your passing,
lambs scurry ewe-wards for safety.

Missed by their mouths,
a purple splash with golden centre,
the Easter Pasque still blooms
from this thin soil.

The hedge drips blossom.
From the shade a fox emerges,
coat glistening sun, and
ambles across the field.

Marking his territory on a tussock,
brush straight behind,
he climbs to the trough in
the wall and drinks his fill.

A ewe calls, her lamb's echo
cuts the close silence.
The distant chorus of
birdsong washes over.

A breeze caresses the hillside
rolling last years leaves
of parchment oak
gently over the sward.

Long shadows of evening
stretch the valley.
Spring has finally come
once more to Cotswold.

Belladonna

You linger at light edge,
hide your dusky enchantment,
still subtly beautiful.

But what luscious black
devil's cherries you flaunt
to lure us to our fate.

We long to fill our mouths
with the tempt of you
yet know we dare not try.

Should you seduce the unwary,
should they succumb, bewitched
by your treacherous charms.

Then, with wide eyes,
accelerated hearts,
pulse weakening,

nerves numbed to oblivion,
they drift into your arms,
waiting, in the shadows.

Keeping station

Hang, effortless,
scatter refracted light.
Waft, deflect current,
slip water over scale.
Mouthe calmness, cool grace.

Flick, propel
rise to passing speck.
Ring surface, sip in,
taste, reject, float up,
drift past on the film.

Sink down to station,
lie by snaking weed,
flow quieter here.
Wait for the next morsel,
watch life stream by.

Open Sesame

Glimpse a view through blurred hedges each time you pass.
Slow, stop at the gate, lean on the five bars, ramshackle.
Look into sea of waving colour at history laid before you.
Grown and harvested for three hundred summers at least.
The hedge has marked the parish boundary for six centuries.
In seventeen seventy two your owner gave you his name.
Ghost of tillage shows in ancient roll of ridge and furrow.

There's no notice saying - Private - Keep out.
Why not climb over, wade waist deep amongst it all.
But something inside says - This is special - stop,
an unwritten law grown over time between you both.
After the hay is cut only the cows are privileged
to roam, crop sweet grass, rest in green oak shade,
share its bounty with the wild creatures that live there.

Once a year, the gate over which you stared so often swings open.
Welcome to a magic landscape of colour, shape and scent.
Tread gingerly between blooms, know that you trample life.
Delicate green veins, shades of deepest purple through to white,
Ragged pink, gold suns, frothing cream plumes.
Deeper in, from twinned leaves, rise green men on spikes.
Deeper still the single pale curve of leaf with reptile tongue.

After you have drunk deeply, cannot take any more,
close the gate softly behind you, for another year.

Gardener

He seeks a seed of a special kind,
finds her trapped in a desert,
wrapped in protective coat
of someone else's making.
Still she waits, clings to life,
struggles to be free.

He takes her gently in his hands,
plants in the bed prepared,
prays she will take root.
Water to sustain, food to nourish,
loving hands guard from harm,
protect her from the storm.

He waits, watches for the signs,
the tender sprout that finds
a way out through the shell.
Up through the grains,
reaching, for the light,
the freedom of life.

He watches her grow and flourish,
finally flower, bear fruit.
Hopes she is perennial,
will not float away on the wind
but stay forever, form
beds that bloom all year.

She is free, the world her pot,
the earth her soil,
the sun her light
and he the gardener
to carry on the fight
lest she should come to any harm.

Midsummer Meeting

Curved steel cuts black hedged tunnel,
grazes warm dark.

Struck from night, tumbled feathers
pluck edge of eye.

The clash screeches, claws through air,
cracks hollow bone.

Sucked from sky, silent wings lash,
flailing the verge.

Head wheels, flashes stunned coal beads,
bundled in sack.

Calm descends, splint and time learns,
to perch again,

launch aloft, grasp the dark night,
plunge in soft vole.

Slipstream

Up where the wind waters eye,
a backdrop of hills, a sinking sun.
Four dark sails slide between clouds,
sweep and glide, scour the view,
drop deep into patchwork green.
A sudden rush, a glimpse, as
black rags flash past from below,
tossed by air streaming up scarp.
Watch as they slip, bank, stall,
tumble from sky, half closed,
split the draught with wings.
Circle on currents, swoop again,
rocket up once more.
Hear air buffet each feather
strain the barbs.
Sheer pleasure of wind
screaming through pinions
brings a deep throaty gurgle,
almost a chuckle, as they revel
in the exhilaration of pure play.

Angle

wade through grass
scuff shine from shoes
acid suck of sorrel
moistens dry mouth
pick a way across
bog from tuft to tuft
past the pump graveyard
from school cross-country

to the rivulet that teems
with loach and minnow
on to the damp depression
that marks the pond where
orange bellied monsters
roam through tangled weed
to common's meandering stream
guarded by creaking willows

strained to the winds tune
thighs of mossy trunks split
and fallen lean over choked pools
beneath whose scummed surface
spotted and barred pike lurk
fin the water waiting
ease through spears of fringing reed
freeze to moorhens loud 'kurruck'

silently curse as it skitters away
the black ooze clings
draws sulphide into air
climb up inch out along branch
rasp of bark and lichen
against skin scratches
clamped legs till they reach
the cool of mossy patch

notch the elder arrow
onto string of garden twine
draw back the willow bow
the trembling hand releases
thin shaft pierces sallow light
calm water explodes boils
wished that we had hit
knew we were wide of the mark

Cedar and Crow

No one remembers how long the cedar has stood
No one recalls when the crow first nested
It has always been so

They were here when I came
the cedar and the crow
they will remain when I go

The stick pile sits astride flattened tree top
added to each year replacing losses
claimed by a season's weather

Caw breaks the calm
Caw raises the alarm
Caw warns intruders

Secure from ground save from marauding squirrel
arced wings swoop, protect from aerial attack
buffet passing Sparrowhawk, harass chattering pie

Heavy in black young flap furiously
tumble down layered branches
of grey-green needles

last year's cones,
standing proud, explode
and rattle to the ground

Youngsters flop in a heap
sidle across grass with ungainly hop
Parents 'Kaah' soft encouragement

Then, you realise by the quiet they have gone,
till the year circles and twig in beak
they return to replay the ritual over again.

BST

Our evening walk changes.
the still light of a setting sun
gilds a widening vapour trail
opposite an Easter egg moon.

Bright in the western sky
the evening star
second planet from the sun
shines from the cobalt blue
above dark clouded horizon.

Bells ring over the river
calm with swans.
Ropes rise and fall
in lighted tower windows.

Under the arch the peal
muffles and deepens
from the other side
swells and sharpens.

Dark to light,
sight and sound.

Spotted

Suddenly you materialise
grace us with your presence
not spring but fat august
a pause on your way south
from under yews deep shade
the intent watchful gaze
with dart - twist - flutter
you outmanoeuvre - capture
the buzz of summer
turn on a feather
return to perch

by instinct or learning
your bright unblinking eye
found this oasis
in a concrete land
you cannot be the same
catcher of flies
a descendant perhaps
but you are here - then
black eye searching
skies for African warmth
just as suddenly - gone

Thorn

My time comes but once a year,
I follow the black and plum,
after my month I am named,
the only one.

I wear sweet trim of white
over my cloak of green,
freshness of petals budded tight,
promise of fruit to come.

My strange odour haunts the air,
smell the lust, taste the decay
that hangs from the hedges
in which I dance on my day.

Quick to grow I keep
the stock at bay, mark
boundaries, enclosures,
places where you meet.

Most celebrate of all,
sprung from Joseph's staff,
stand on the hill of Wearyall,
grace queen's table at Christmastide.

But you,
you must never
cast a clout till I am out
and never take me in.

Plum

Every year you come
brave the burn of icy nights
blast of western gale
batter of hail, even
the smother of snow.
White tender frailty
turns to tiny fruitlet
green on the twig.
Grow in warming sun
swell and colour, soften
as you reach your prime.
Ripe, plucked from branch
fresh from the tree
a season's sweet juice oozes
sticks the hand that picks.
Teeth sink into silky flesh
the taste pure nectar,
fills the mouth, dribbles
down the chin.

Mute

Beneath your own stars wings,
drift over unruffled dark
perform 'swan et lumiere'.

Breasting the flow that
sparkles in streetlights
you come with curved grace.

Tear bread piece by piece,
serrated edge rasps fingers,
feel for notch, royal or not?

Half heard, your call echoes
over water, cuts the
observed silence, brings others

that ghost from the gloom,
too late, they drift into night,
ripples dying to calm.

Dress in feathers white,
become the maiden pure,
sing the fabled song.

You saw the body in the water,
the flowers on the bank,
but pass no comment.

Cycle

Stand stark and bare
darkened by the rain
deep within fluids rise
through cell and tube again
swell the bud that bursts
after winter purges clean

From each and every branch
glow bright for all to see
open to the frost and gale
that scatters from the tree
finally you brown and die
then turns the tree to green

Pale mint you brave sharp air
work long the summer through
turn good of earth and sun to
sweet fruit touched with dew
when autumn comes harvest yield
as winds once more blow keen

Leaves yellow gold and brown
blacken as they decay
rest under another cloak of white
sleep harsh cold away then
wear once more your magic coat
spring white upon the scene

Place

Where is this place, where I was born,
this midland shire, this market town.
This green garden upon the hill
to which I am rooted,
from which I have grown.

The soft contours of the Avon valley
flanked by Bredon's dome.
Where the Vale blossom snows,
Cotswold beeches sigh on the ridge,
the Severn meadows silver with flood,
the cropped grass bleaches over Malvern rock.

It is here, I am home.

About the Author

Born & bred & still living in the Vale of Evesham
Bob Woodroofe's poems appear in many poetry
magazines & are performed locally. Inspired by
the natural world, the landscape & local tradition
he attempts to bring the magic of nature & its
restorative & healing qualities to a wider audience.

Also available from the

Greenwood Press
38 Birch Avenue
Evesham
Worcs. WR11 1YJ

website http://greenwoodpress.co.uk

e-mail info@greenwoodpress.co.uk

by Bob Woodroofe

A trilogy of poetry collections from
life & nature in the Vale of Evesham

Nature, Reflections & Spirit of the Vale

In search of greenness

Something Stirred

the Poetry Collection

Pick of the crop

Joint poetry collections by
Sue Johnson & Bob Woodroofe

Tales of Trees & **Journey**

Creative Writing books
by Sue Johnson

Writer's Toolkit
&
Writer's Toolkit 2, 3 & 4

www.ingramcontent.com/pod-product-compliance
Ingram Content Group UK Ltd.
Pitfield, Milton Keynes, MK11 3LW, UK
UKHW041643190726
13854UKWH00006B/2668

9 780952 116523